EARTH DAYS

POEMS, CHANTS, & SPELLS

Praise for
ANNIE FINCH'S PREVIOUS WORKS

Annie Finch's poetry is a pure tone that calls us home to the first impulse of poetry. We link to mystery. We lift off.

—Joy Harjo

Like an Olympic ice skater, Annie Finch makes intricate music look smooth and easy. . .I recommend her with enthusiasm—and awe.

—Molly Peacock, President Emerita, Poetry Society of America

"I can state, with absolutely no doubt whatsoever, that Annie Finch taught me to discover the music in my own body. I have never encountered again someone so unflinchingly passionate about the art of poetry and so dedicated to its potential.

—Patricia Smith, National Poetry Award Winner

Annie Finch's poems are at once a continuation and a critique of the plural traditions from which they are drawn, a commentary on the seductive and treacherous—and redemptive—qualities of language itself.

—Marilyn Hacker

Annie Finch's poetry emboldens the spirit and enlightens the soul, offering the listener a journey like no other.

—Jeffrey Cantrell

"In words that soar but are never obscure, Annie Finch tells of Goddesses who have returned offering threads of meaning with which to weave our lives anew. Sing to us, dear Muse."

—Carol P. Christ, author of Rebirth of the Goddess

An oracle, an ecstatic maenad: that is the kind of traditional poet Annie Finch is. Finch, at the forefront of the re-evaluation of traditional form in poetry, uses poetic structures to distract monkey mind so that wild mind sings through. . . she finds rhyme and meter rooted in the oral tradition with its pagan proletarian values. She takes back the master's tools by remembering that they were, from the first, tools of the common folk.

—**Patricia Monaghan,** author of The Women's Encyclopedia of Myths and Secrets

Annie Finch understands better than any contemporary I know what poetry feels like and sounds like when it is completely at home in its traditions. . . .. She is a major poet, one of very few who understand how lyric lives in part because it can speak for something larger than the ego.

—**Charles Altieri,** University of California, Berkeley

Annie Finch is an American original, a master of control who shows no fear of excess, and none of quietness either. . . The directness and simplicity of her poems are deceptive –they have depths and delights that appear to go on forever.

—**Ron Silliman**

Finch is a poet in her bones . . .again and again, I found myself shocked with pleasure as image, idea, and sound spun out in a perfect braid.

—**C.L. Rawlins**

Gnomic, intricate, lyrical, and deft, Finch's poetry brings Dickinson's to mind. . . a poetry that technically precise, that risky and spectacular.

—**C. G. MacDonald,** *San Francisco Poetry Flash*

Annie Finch has made form a one-eyed woman looking out at us all, beckoning us to enter into her arena and be.

—**Sonia Sanchez**

The brightest liveliest most gifted person of her generation . . . Whenever I get discouraged about some trends in American poetry, I think of Annie Finch, a shining light, and I feel better.

—**Carolyn Kizer**

Nirala Series

EARTH DAYS

Annie Finch is an American poet, writer, translator, and speaker known for her incantatory poetry, composed to be read aloud. She is the author of six books of poetry including *Spells: New and Selected Poems, Eve,* and *Calendars* (both finalists for the National Poetry Series), and *Among the Goddesses: An Epic Libretto in Seven Dreams* (awarded the Sarasvati Award). She has also published numerous books about poetry including *A Poet's Craft, The Ghost of Meter, The Body of Poetry,* and nine anthologies on poetics including *A Formal Feeling Comes, Villanelles, An Exaltation of Forms,* and *Measure for Measure: An Anthology of Poetic Meters.* Her poetry has appeared in the *New York Times, Poetry Magazine, Paris Review, Penguin Book of Twentieth-Century American Poetry,* and *Norton Anthology of World Literature* and has been translated into Arabic, Chinese, Farsi, French, Portuguese, Polish, Russian, and Spanish. In 2012 she was awarded the Robert Fitzgerald Award for her lifetime contribution to the Art and Craft of Versification. Finch's verse plays and Poetry Witch Theater rituals have been produced at venues including The Metropolitan Museum of Art, Carnegie Hall, Deepak Chopra Homespace, and American Opera Projects. Educated at Yale University and Stanford University, where she earned her Ph.D, she has performed her poems cross the U.S. and in India, Mexico, Africa, and throughout Europe.

EARTH DAYS

POEMS, CHANTS, & SPELLS IN FIVE DIRECTIONS

Annie Finch

Nirala

Nirala Publications
Third Floor, 310, Hari Sadan,
Daryaganj, New Delhi-110002
niralabooks@yahoo.co.in, niralapublications@gmail.com
www.niralapublications.com

First Edition 2024

ISBN : 978-81-963601-1-5

Cover Art: Annie Finch

Author Photo : Kim Bridgford

Printed at
Chaman Offset New Delhi-2

For M.E.R.

Contents

Part One

FIRE

Part Two

AIR

Part Three

EARTH

Part Four

WATER

Part Five

MATRIX

One
FIRE

Earth Day

All we want is to find the love
in the faces of the people we love.
All we need is to find the dark
in the nighttime sky, to lie down to sleep
in the darkness, where stars and moon keep vigil,
in the silence of a sleeping earth.
All we require is to wake to sunlight
in the morning, to simple sky,
to breathe aloud as the sky is breathing,
to drink the water of the earth.

All we need is to touch the planet
and find it clean where we were born,
where our ancestors breathed and planted,
where we live with the plants and birds.

All we need is to live with the memory
of a future we want to imagine.
All we want is to find the love
in the face of the planet we love.

Summer Solstice Chant

June 21

The sun, rich and open,
stretches and pours on the bloom of our work.

In the center of the new flowers,
a darker wing of flower

points you like a fire.

Point your fire like a flower.

Encounter

Then, in the bus where strange eyes are believed to burn
down into separate depths, ours mingled, lured
out of the crowd like wings--and as fast, as blurred.
We brushed past the others and rose. We had flight to learn,
single as wings, till we saw we could merge with a turn,
arching our gazing together. We formed one bird,
focussed, attentive. Flying in silence, we heard
the air past our feathers, the wind through our feet, and the churn
of wheels in the dark. Now we have settled. We move
calmly, two balanced creatures. Opened child,
woman or man, companion with whom I've flown
through this remembering, lost, incarnate love,
turning away, we will land, growing more wild
with solitude, more alone, than we could have known.

A Blessing for the Poets

Patient earth-digger, impatient fire-maker,
Hungry word-taker and roving sound-lover,
Sharer and saver, muser and acher,
You who are open to hide or uncover,
Time-keeper and –hater, wake-sleeper, sleep-waker;
May language's language, the silence that lies
Under each word, move you over and over,
Turning you, wondering, back to surprise.

Architecture

Proportion is life measured open by harmony.
It vaults us to open like atriums, entering
our pillared awareness in footsteps, then building
our spaces with conscious decision. Its mystery
makes earth that our forest looks back for. Its beauty
has felt us repeating, then come to repeat us.
Its answers have carved us like mineral and bent us
in spirals. Its questions have rocked us past symmetry.
And, if we have voices that build to a word
and breathe out through poems, it comes to enclose us
by seeding the places we know we inhabit—
(make local, remember, name, touch and are stirred
in, share with those who understand, love, or oppose us
(because they live here, in the place we inhabit,
and believe what we have grown wise believing:
that belief, like love, rests on no foundation
but the shapes we know how to make by knowing
how they enclose us))—
how they unfold us.

Homebirth

For Vincent

Home is a birthplace since you came to me,
pouring yourself down through me like a soul,
calling the cosmos imperiously
into me so it could reach to unroll
out from the womb where the wild rushes start
in a quick, steady heartbeat not from my own heart.
This is my body, which you made to break,
which gave you to make you, till you bear its mark,
which held you till you found your body to take,
(open at home on my bed in the dark).

The Menstrual Hut

How can I listen to the moon?
Your blood will listen, like a charm.

I knew a way to feel the sun
as if a statue felt warm eyes.
Even with ruins on the moon,
your blood will listen, every time.

Now I am the one with eyes.
Your blood can listen, every time.

Running in Church

for Marie

Then, you were a hot-thinking, thin-lidded tinderbox.
Losing your balance meant nothing at all. You would
pour through the aisles in the highest cathedrals,
careening deftly as patriarchs brooded.

You made the long corridors ring, tintinnabular
echoes exploring the pounded cold floor,
forcing the walls to the truth of your progress:
there was a person in this church's core.

Past thick stained-glass colors wafted and swirling
in pooled interludes that swung down from the rafters,
cinnabar wounds threw light on your face, where the
pliant young bones were dissolving in laughter.

Zaraf's Star

Walking changes as dusk starts to gather.
We're not able or sure anymore.
We don't know the path--and if we did know it,

we wouldn't go on. We're afraid of the dark
lowering its heavy, long familiarity
down on the grass. We're afraid of the night,

moonless, desert, California,
making us stumble. We shouldn't be lost,
out here like demons just at the border

that touches us solid, as if we were gone.
She's leading me on a path as narrow
as sisters can share. We pound back down the mesa.

Each of our feet finds its own way, delving
into the gulley whose trees never answer
until, with steps slapping soft as bandits,

I slow on the path, imagining horses.

Stretching necks right out of the stones,
out of the dusk where dark has achieved our
bodies, drawn by the strides that my sister

takes like a rider, Zaraf's Star,
Fashad, Kashmir, Arabian horses
raise her up with motionless shadow

so she can ride (like a rider, she walks),
cantering, encompassing the pace of the mountain.
Out in a landscape to curl or be curled in,

hunched like riders or curling like rides,
under the fairy-tale oaks of the mesa
that hide sleeping children or horses inside,

we talk about horses like hers who run carefully,
with thinner ankles, and mustangs who, fast,
wild grown, wild on the path to blackness,

hunger like stars reaching down for dark leaves.

Strangers

She turned to gold and fell in love.
She danced life upside down.

She opened her eyes again
and asked some strangers in.

The strangers felt her in and out.
They found her outsides thin.

Since her heart was still and hurt,
they knocked her insides in.

In Cities, Be Alert

You may hear that your heartbeat is uneven
and let new tension climb around your shoulders,
thinking you've found the trick for going mad.
But try to keep a grip on where you are.

Remember: all around you is pure city;
try to stay alert. On the wide streets,
so empty late at night, streaking in glass,
the color of an alley, or the fall

of a sideways flicker from a neon sign
may utterly and briefly disconcert you—
but as you go, you'll find that noise is worse.
Prepare for noise. But never scream. Even tensing

ears too far in advance can sharpen sirens,
and as for horns. . .. When you're back to
your normal rhythm after such encounters,

just try to stay alert. You'll never know
exactly who is coming up behind you,
but the sudden movement of pedestrians
will finally, of course, be what disarms you.

Now in November

Now in November, as I face towards home
pulling my living behind me, and my dead,
the skulls of fire widen into a road.
November turns into a room of leaves
and lets them fall around him. Then he goes,
and where he stood, his body blank and bare,
only a halo of shocked twigs remains
spread on the still green, still elusive grass.

Inside the Violet

Beside the long hedge on my parents' drive,
where the gravel waited daily for their tires
to crunch it open, in the narrow band
of earth along the hedge that kept the loam's
thick secret from the shifting sun, I knew
a purple violet. It always grew there,
hanging its knotty shoulders in the shade
of large, more splendid leaves, its crumpled head
releasing toward the earth.

One day I crouched
to find its eye much closer than before
and stared inside. My own eye was lost
in the echoing hold of the raw deep I saw,
though my hands held back inside the driveway world
that slowed its pulse around me as loud sun
shattered all the gravel into shade
and stroked the earth. The middle of the violet loomed;
its heart was peeking into me to hold
me like a violet, too. As its yellow, strong
throat turned to me and opened like a door,
interior light poured from a silent sun,
flooding my face and choking my eyes, until
I stopped looking in violets.

Westminster

Among these aisles and these attentive pews,
as sunset lowers silk down through the shafts
of remembering light, your whispering voice calls

from the stone bed, where long-resounding rose
embroiders the marble bodies as you plead,
"It's not my face; take this pocked stone away."

The other soldiers still hold the stiff lances
of their endless sight-lines to the roof. But I
have seen your crumbling life. You need to die.

I read the ruthless carvings on the low
Scherezades of monuments--designed
to run the reader through with Latin words--

looming always, waiting, drawing drying tears
to halo lead and stone. Dust writes the huge
cold pages pushing, with silent black and gold,

toward your tumble of marble sheets. One-armed, you lie
beside your husband, your thinning fingers spread
on your crumbled nipple, waiting for the stone

and time to cover them. The stone will kneel.
Here, silt-heart kings and sand-bodied dukes,
holding lead in the church, and dark in your hands,

the dead time is over. There is no life here;
My night is abandoning the night where you lie,
where she and he walked up an aisle to He.

My Raptor

My mind hovered over my baby, like
a raptor, and froze everything it saw.
I looked through my own pregnant belly's raw
perimeters and found his heart to strike
attentive until, helpless with the pound
of still more blood, he seemed to settle down.
It was my loss to feel like god alone
for a new one always listening, to reach
inside for his ears to share the flying speech
I heard so constantly. Within my grown
silence, my sounding, my loud body where
the baby turned, my mind learned not to care
whether thoughts I felt he noticed with no fear
were mine alone—or whether he could hear.

First Poem

The honest spirit
is bewildered
by the going of the night.
Bruised back by morning's light squares, she laments:

> I've settled in a clan of waking ghosts.
> There's no more solid thing for me than light.

But here the flick of evening opens
her who let stars' spider trails
run quick cold sticky errands through her night.

Day breaks into a pomegranate,
or some night of leaping patterns,
and she breaks to hear your words,
and now she's dialogue:

> Attent me! Let the syntax crack!
>
> > My voice in an old tangle of synapse . . .
>
> You will tug at the old strains daily
>
> > I'm a mirror, and a sieve

So sift and scald the ancient cups. Don't sleep.
Give your blanched filters back for homage.

Nightmare

Opening light calls the river back to see
where the old nightmare has risen from, when she
calls herself back in the rhythm that is she.
Nightmare, oh woman lost in the depths of me,
lost to the rage that has risen up with me,
lost till I ride you home--nightmare of me.

Wild Yeasts

Rumbling a way up my dough's heavy throat to its head,
seeping the trailed, airborne daughters down into the core,
bubbles go rioting through my long-kneaded new bread;
softly, now, breath of the wildest yeast starts to roar.
My hands work the peaked foam, push insides out into the light,
edge shining new sinews back under the generous arch
that time's final sigh will conclude. (Dry time will stretch tight
whistling stops of quick heat through my long-darkened starch.)

How could I send quiet through this resonant, strange, vaulting roof
murmuring, sounding with spores and the long-simple air,
and the bright free road moving? I sing as I terrace a loaf
out of my hands it has filled like a long-answered prayer.
Now the worshipping savage cathedral our mouths make will lace
death and its food, in the moment that refracts this place.

Lucid Waking

Once I wanted the whole dawn not to let me
sleep. One morning, then, I awoke and watched as
waking woke me, came slipping up through half-light
crying softly, a cat leaving her corner,
stretching, tall in the new gray air of morning,
raising paws much too high. She came slow-stepping
down the hallway to crouch, to call, to answer
through the door, making still and slow the dawning
once so bird-ridden—and the sun, the curtains—

Imbolc Chant

February 1

From the east she has gathered like wishes.
She has woven a night into dawn.
We are quickening ivy. We grow
where her warmth melts out over the ice.

Now spiral south bends into flame
to push the morning over doors.
The light swings wide, green with the pulse
of seasons, and we let her in

We are quickening ivy. We grow

The light swings wide, green with the pulse

till the west is rocked by darkness
pulled from where the fire rises.
Shortened time's reflecting water
rakes her through the thickened cold.

Hands cover north smooth with emptiness,
stinging the mill of night's hours.
Wait with me. See, she comes circling
over the listening snow to us.

Shortened time's reflecting water

Wait with me. See, she comes circling

Churching

(The several weeks after childbirth when a woman was considered unclean and was not allowed to attend church)

Covered with the latitudes of war,
and holding up the blood of my own son

(earth and the water surround you. So I surround you,
leaf over water, stem over stone)

keeping the dark urgency of the long night
I will not go into your church

(scalloped by moons)

I stay here looking at my own blood
(on both sides)
I stay here holding up my blood
(simultaneously)
I will stand here with my own blood
(in adopting forests)

Black and slippery, rusty and strong,
prolific and arching out through my thick hair,
(The hugest, completest old planets are twisting around you)

fervent and striking, aimed at the land
(So you bask alive)

here is my power-blood,

(in the simplest sun)

fruits of my land

my own country

(Reaching through a gate)

This is the blood that came out of the fullness
that grows in me like a forest
(To narrow)
of trees so strong

(or hold)

so much taller than I am
(while spending)

so much dark greener than I am

(to)
Here is this fullness.
(form).

The church is in me, the church of the tall trees.

Paravaledellentine: A Paradelle

For Glen

Come to me with your warning sounds of the tender seas.
Come to me with your warning sounds of the tender seas.
Move me the way the seas' warm sea will spend me.
Move me the way the seas' warm sea will; spend me.
Move your sea-warm come to me; will with me; spend
tender sounds, warning me the way of the seas, the seas.

Tongues sharp as two wind-whipped trees will question.
Tongues sharp as two wind-whipped trees will question.
(Skin or nerve waiting and heart will answer.
Skin or nerve waiting and heart will answer).
Question will answer two tongues and, or will:
heart sharp as nerve trees; waiting, skin-whipped wind.

Brim your simple hand over where the skin is.
Brim your simple hand over where the skin is.
Wish again, whenever hair and breath come closer.
Wish again, whenever hair and breath come closer.
Closer, again, whenever; brim where your skin is;
hair, wish and breath over the simple hand, come.

Spend come warning me, whenever simple sounds will, will;
move your question. Answer your heart-sharp tender
sea-warm will with me. Way of the seas, the seas!
Where skin-whipped nerve trees wind over waiting tongues,
brim closer to me. Again the skin, as wish,
and two of the breath, hand and hair, or come, is.

A Valentine for Hands

For Glen

names, silence—quietest minutes
(building like rain or returning like seas)
since they have touched me, your warm hands have sown
gentlest sounds, touches and hours
(or, building like rain, turning, like seas)

(building like rain, or returning like seas)
ripples and springs—the shiniest rivers—
since they have known me your warm hands have gathered
smallest, most stars—happiest skies—
simplest—touched—sounding—hours

Revelry

For Sitwells Cafe

Chairs root. Their trunks are runged with snow.
Curtains grow velvet thick, like bark,
in this warm landscape ringed with dark.
Is passion only revelry?

Voices believe words and move free.
Lust moves our lips. Blood fills our skin.
We bend alive around cup and cloud.
These are the hours to revel in.

Two
AIR

Early Chant

Crabs, sea-shells, white ants, cats,
A budding, a maple,
Iron, Mint, wind starting.

Hills, birthing, seedling, root,
Rust, quiet, noise, hearing,
Crabs, sea-shells, white ants, cats.

Bay, webs, shells, foaling, milk,
Sap rising, fog, copper,
Iron, mint, wind starting.

Short thunder, open mouth,
Itch, billow, moon growing,
Crabs, sea-shells, white ants, cats.

Track, ripple, jolt, clay, touch,
A howling, a call, sheep,
Iron, mint, wind starting.

Air, rising, dying, leaf,
Beast, mouse, worm, what started,
Crabs, sea-shells, white ants, cats,
Iron, mint, wind starting.

Moon

Then are you the dense everywhere that moves,
the dark matter they haven't yet walked through?

No, I'm not. I'm just the shining sun,
sometimes covered up by the darkness.

But in your beauty—yes, I know you see—
There is no covering, no constant light.

Being A Constellation

Heavy with my milk, you move
your compact body, though I hold
you dense under a constellation
whose sparse lights ache over you.

If, looking up, you recognize
the shadowing of curves that casts
towards my belly, and the way
my nipples travel, like two stars

twinned by your eyesight; if my arms
take night, and keep it from the sky,
if my night voice can stop your cry,
I'll be the Mother over you.

You are a question, small and dense,
and I am an answer, long diffuse
and dark, but I want to be sky
for you so, like the stars, I lie,

holding my far lights wide and flat
in pictures for your eyes to take,
spaced easily, so you can catch
the patterns in your sleepy net.

A Crown of Leaves for Moneta

September 21

Our voices press
from us
and twine
around the year's
fermenting wine

Yellow fall roars
Over the ground.
Loud, in the leafy sun that pours
Liquid through doors,
Yellow, the leaves twist down

as the winding
of the vine
pulls our curling
voices—

Glowing in wind and change,
The orange leaf tells

How one more season will alter and range,
Working the strange
Colors of clamor and bells

In the winding
of the vine
our voices press out
from us
to twine

When autumn gathers, the tree
That the leaves sang

Reddens dark slowly, then, suddenly free,
Turns like a key,
Opening air where they hang

and the winding
of the vine
makes our voices
turn and wind
with the year's
fermented wine

One of the hanging leaves,
Deeply maroon,
Tightens its final hold, receives,
Finally weaves
Through, and is covered soon

in the winding
of the vine—

Holding past summer's hold,
Open and strong,
One of the leaves in the crown is gold,
Set in the cold
Where the old seasons belong.

Here is my crown
Of winding vine,
Of leaves that dropped,
That fingers twined,
another crown
to yield and shine
with a year's
fermented wine.

Caribou Kitchen

Most things have vanished
while we were talking
(the dents in a pitcher
gleam by the gas lamp),
but nothing is lost
(cups in far corners).
Arms still lean
over the table
(shadows on the oilcloth).

Without a Bird

This is a dawn
without a sun

(that has no birds)

This is a dawn
that will not part

(that will not sing)

Night has no birds
that will not sing

(out of this cold)

This is a dawn
This is a dawn

(that is not spring)

Butterfly Lullaby

My wild indigo dusky wing
my mottled, broad-wing skipper,
a sleepy, dreamy dusty wing,
flying through my night.

My northern, southern, cloudy wing,
my spring azure, my crescent pearl,
a silver-spotted, sweet question mark,
sleeping in my sky.

A tiger swallowtail, harvester,
moving through my hours,
an eyed brown in the redwing dark,
wrapped softly in my words.

The Door

It seemed as if a door came calling,
in a voice as old as carols,
telling lies as old as candles,
in words that were all about
some afternoons, lost on a child,
that could have been simple but
were lost, when I was just a child.

There was a day and then a dream
that I went through, and a cathedral
whose tall choir prayed
a singing message through the nave
until I heard a forest there
(though far outside, the trees were bare)

Belly

"So seems this life on earth, compared with the time that is unknown to us: as if you sat feasting with your thanes in wintertime, with a fire burning, and your hall warm, and it rained and snowed and stormed outside; and a sparrow quickly flew through that house, in through one of the doors, and out through the other. " —Bede

Humming sparrow touching my breast
from deep in the dark,

belly turns one voice open in this place of clouds,
charming, and tethered by deep in the dark.

Sparrow who is coming, looking for rest,
from deep in the dark,

belly reaps winter open in one flying charm,
tree and belief, heavy fish-rushing spark

of mother and daughter, husband and son,
from deep in the dark,
from deep in the dark.

Sapphics for Patience

Look there—something rests on your hand and even
lingers, though the wind all around is asking
it to leave you. Passing the windy passage,
you have been chosen.

Seed. Like dust or thistle, it sits so lightly
that your hand while holding the trust of silk gets
gentle. Seed like hope has come, making stillness.
Wish, in the quiet.

If I stood there—stopped by a windy passage—
staring at my hand—which is always open—
hopeful, maybe, not to compel you, I'd wish
only for patience.

Iowa Barn

Light and shadow
frame a window
that comes reaching
past a roof-edge
and becomes a hole. Sky goes
funneling to
any darkness,
cut by warped
wooden framing,
long-abandoned
by the glass that
could reflect us.

Three Generations of Secrets

Is the sound of my loud carrying life a knell
far across your small ocean? Do you share
the secret that the months keep hidden there?
Is my past-filled pregnancy a hungry shell?
I think I will turn metal, like a bell,
so you can clapper my voice out, to where
the silent memories will echo care
and speak again. We'll sound our double spell,
swinging; we'll swing back then, to forgive
my mother's curve around the angry past—
and then her mother's. They were smothered, bound
and quiet. But we'll speak, and you will live,
tolling and striking what we know at last,
until you ring aloud with newer sounds.

The Coming Mirrors

My body thickens in a stem
climbing aloud to keep you here.

My belly thickens like a stem,
my belly is tethered by your days.

Come in, come in, my strong darling.
I'm still a pane of airy glass.

My breasts go heavy to meet you here.

My body turns in place of clouds,
I grow like a pane of open glass.

My body is a forest floor
where needles blend to keep you here.
My belly thickens like a stem.

Come in, come in, my last darling,
and let the coming mirrors pass.

The Intellect of Woman

"The intellect of man is forced to choose
perfection of the life or of the work."
—Yeats, "The Choice"

The intellect of woman must not choose
perfection of the life, or of the work.
Perfection has a diamond for a muse
who scratches where she only needs to look.

And yet the intellect of woman fears
imperfection's lonely grandeur where the sharp
delight of knowing presses through her ears,
the blade's edge cuts her vision through the dark.

So the intellect of woman will not mind
some scratches where the diamond's edge has moved.
Perfection's habit opens us to find
cuts in a window we have never loved.

Blue Willow

Once days blew in a pattern, when blue willows
bent where they blew, and bowls filled with birds
and plates arched out from them. Days blew across cups,
and covered the stories on saucers, and then the week came.

It's morning. Day rises above me,
and my own house, and the door, the tea in the cup
that you sip from, the blue willow china,
till more sun leans over the backs of the chairs—

Insect

That hour-glass-backed,
orchard-legged,
heavy-headed will,

paper-folded,
wedge-contorted,
savage—dense to kill—

pulls back on backward-moving,
arching
high legs still,

lowered through a deep, knees-reaching,
feathered down
green will,

antenna-honest,
thread-descending,
carpeted as if with skill,

a focus-changing,
sober-reaching,

tracing, killing will.

Final Autumn

Maple leaves turn black in the courtyard.
Light drives lower and one bluejay crams
our cold memories out past the sun,

each time your traces come past the shadows
and visit under my looking-glass fingers
that lift and block out the sun.

Come—I'll trace you one final autumn,
and you can trace your last homecoming
into the snow or the sun.

The Circled Sand

Oaks have thickened. Blackberries
untighten. Warmed stones
encircle the dense and swerving sand.

Years, and weeks and hours,
have turned, while water lily petals
hid the surface, then submerged,
or got tangled in our paddles.

Maple hands pushed their green light through you.
Then the pine and maple trees moved past,
the water opened out,
and mist appeared on the water.

The Wish for Eyes

On solid hills through liquid dusk,
the city turns to rise

with its purple touch, to enter me.
I touch it with my eyes.

Righted with wrongs, or even hard,
Let me be made of eyes.

Gray nature, make a dusk of me,
and let me keep my ties.

Frozen in

Venice, December

Ours are the only mouths
to taste with this smothering slow
touch, and the only steps
to sink like bellsounds and cave
deep into the marble snow.

Women who go to the window
to push their arms out to the snow
and then bring the shutters back in
follow us as we fall
past their eyes where the black night lives.

We are snowflakes at last, as the thick
never locked, never closed doors
follow us through squares of light
their windows have left on the snow.
Once again, warmth that falls,
again, though our tracks fill and slow.

A Way to See

Line to line
the framings move
Window through window
through eyes.

Lake's water
moves through the house
Meets me in garden
all arched.

House is to
wall a window
with cup or a web
on sill.

Sill and pane
the framings move
Arched and glassed, they make
Complete.

Winter Solstice Chant

December 21

Vines, leaves, roots of darkness, growing,
now you are uncurled and cover our eyes
with the edge of winter sky
leaning over us in icy stars.
Vines, leaves, roots of darkness, growing,
come with your seasons, your fullness, your end.

Speak Softly

The birds are everywhere, and hardly sing,
and I am anywhere, an only thing
(speak softly, and we do not own the land):

a thin wind settled, spored on cotton sand,
and convoluted. Wind over the land.
The birds are everywhere, and hardly sing.

I am a settler who was settled here
to speak and have no words about this land.
Its touch is built on shreds of spoken sand.

Its beat tells in sad bound and open hands.
Its old words sing in words my ears can't hear,
since they were spoken here, not anywhere,

and I am anywhere, an only thing,
while birds are everywhere, and hardly sing,
and my home fills me up with touching hands
I cannot touch—that never owned the land.

Two Bodies

Two bodies, balanced in mass and power,
move in a bed through the dark,
under the earliest human hour.
A night rocks, like an ark.

They reach through the ceilings of the night,
tall as animals.
Through their valleys bends the light
of their fertile hills.

Two bodies breathe their close hellos
through interlocking pores,
while that hush of beating slows,
held, with many oars,

heart over heart, leg over leg,
trading still breath, until,
heart over heart, and seed into egg,
night holds two bodies still.

Three
EARTH

Meeting Mammoth Cave, Eight Months Pregnant

With my dark eyes open,
I search into the dark
for a reassurance
to soothe me like a look.

No beam will sink or angle,
no slow new mineral drip
through the circling ceiling,
no change of quiet drop.

Her womb will throw me outward
(unbreakably deep kiss),
inhospitable, solid,
into no circumference,

carrying dark to hold me,
to empty the slippery
solid cavern's holding,
to hollow the beautiful

loud strength of a darkness
only dark can reassure,
in the night to my humanness
the unparticled has poured.

The Garden

Out of old earth that the worms ate,
the grim garden began to grow.
Peas, like dull dragons, unwound and dipped
rough leaves that the land had licked,

lulled by a lingering dust of crumbs
left by the tongue of the turned-up
underground earth. Over the dirt,
beans bent their bowed figureheads,

Bent so heavy, held so hard,
That it filled them with force to face furrows
through the wind. They'll walk waves.

Mowing

Easing the land into one long-plotted scene,
we stroke the grass into piles with the rake.
Earth's face goes quiet, moved to a docile green
tinge blushed for other eyes, not for our sake.
Harrow the lawn, pack leaves of grass to loam,
flatten the seed-tall walls that would twist and sigh
around us, carve down the rooted caves that foam
with causeless silence, kill the lace-long sky.
Why harvest a grain whose worth is to remain,
ignore the seeds, leaving the yield unkept,
trudging lost kernels to such empty gain?
Won't this world reap until we've stopped and swept
all the harvest away? Must we stand to see
this land lie plain, its hands open and empty?

Mbote, Kinshasa

Kinshasa, warm city spread out and alive,
Night-dark in rich silence, bird-bright in rich sun,
Kinshasa, deep heartbeat, strong, ready to give,
Kinshasa, the many, Kinshasa, the one.

Night-dark in rich silence, bird-bright in rich sun,
You nourish the voices your country will need.
Kinshasa, the many, Kinshasa, the one,
You offer the stars of your brightness like seed.

You nourish the voices your country will need.
Kinshasa, warm city spread out and alive
You offer the stars of your brightness like seed,
Kinshasa, the many, Kinshasa, the one.

Conversation

Edward Weston's "Squash," 1936

"Delve for me, delve down, delve past your body, crowned
by its hidden stem, like a shadowy alarm;
see how you vanish past our dark-shed charm,
throat over throat, ankle to ankle, bound
in our different arches, summer-nicked and browned
interlocking rings in the chain of wrist and arm."

"Lie for me, lie. I want to feel you turn.
Mark out the summer's bending month and learn
to cradle the concrete ground till it softens. Stay.
Measure me past my stem. Though your shadows churn,
close yourself over. Encompass me like clay."

Earth Goddess and Sky God

You haven't formed me. I'm a monster still.

Then give me your body. Give it to me in rain.

Look up and fill me. I am too dark to stain.

You haven't held me. I hold apart my will

Spread dryness through me. I have a night to fill

in high heat-speckled waves, apart from where

I will come down. I have nothing to share

with breath. I will give it back. There is one to kill,

one to renew, and one to persuade to weep.

My night holds everything except for sleep.

When Daphne Ran

When Daphne ran, leaving the god to stand,
Holding his useless arrows in his hand,
To stand, to run, and reach the forming tree
Just quickly enough to watch and touch the last
Dissolving into wood of the now steadfast
And rooted flesh, did she mean to flee
Really away from his huge and glorious hand,
Leaving him really, baffled and shining, to stand?
She had hated how he kicked his way through the wood,
Knowing a few of his low singing words would seduce
Her, calling his lust, letting his love loose
On her, big and imperious, crowding the trembling wood,
Till she suddenly ran, and he stopped for a second to stand.
The wood was still; he stared at his trembling hand.
She, still in the night, long after the god has gone,
Taking his tears, his lyre, his laurel wreath,
She, her mind growing vague already beneath
The layers of bark, vaguely remembering dawn,
Vaguely remembers: by dawn she'll forget the bright hand,
And the last way he touched her, before he left her to stand.

Chain of Women

These are the seasons Persephone promised
as she turned on her heel;
the ones that darken, till green no longer
bandages what I feel—

Now touches of gold stipple the branches,
promising weeks of time
to fade through, finding the footprints
she left as she turned to climb.

Forest Falling

Under the leaves where you'd be lying,
life makes woods of Tennessee
as leaves and loam grow down, drying
brown from chlorophyll and tree.
Needles that loosen, where you'd be,
range to the ground or graze down
the tunneled heights so quietly
they have not gathered. On the ground,
under the needles where earth would like you to break
        and drown,

tunnels fill the earth like foam,
the sentried, calm land breaks down,
and fungi blacken into loam.
Would seas of insects wash those brown
and buttressed skies with catacombs?
Would leaves the trees gave up to spin
through the teeth of their waiting, branching comb
weave you back again? You would begin
to rot into those trees whose forest we have been,

where root hair cells would take you in,
where I'd thread through if I could break
out from the trees that forest in
my branch with leaves, where I would
make ground for the earth if I could,
take sounds of all your unheard trying
down with me to fall, and break,
ranging the tunnels that are only dying,
circling so slowly, circling them, and crying.

Lamia to Lycius

"A serpent!" echoed he; no sooner said
than with a frightful scream she vanished
and Lycius' arms were empty of delight,
as were his limbs of life, from that same night.
— John Keats, "Lamia"

Do you hear me, Lycius? Do you hear these dreams
moving like words out of the air, it seems?
You think you saw me thin into a ghost,
impaled by his old eyes, with their shuddering boast
of pride that kills truth with philosophy.
But you hear this voice. It is a serpent's, or
is it a woman's, this a rich-emblazoned core
reaching out loud for you, as I once reached
for you with clinging hands, and held you, and beseeched?
I had a woman's tears, and woman's teeth
that could not bite, although the ruddy wreath
of my soft lips was closing. And my heart
crawled like a serpent. And that is the part
you married, Lycius, when you made the sun
shine over my damp earth, and grew with me to one
(I had thought our love was closer than belief,
palpable to outwit such stinging grief).
Now in the empty air, as our mouths grow slow,
open your ears to a voice that will never know
your cold and subtle school's philosophy.
Then speak to me, with your body's memory.

To the African Violets

These words and I don't see you, though we charge
like horses past your tumid living stems,
stepping behind our braided forelocks, down
the paths your stems make, rooting underground.

Our tails move last into the mossy dirt,
swishing the last light of daylight off.
How else could we approach? I knew I'd end
with winding, deep inside such patient caves.

Ancestor

Grizzel McNaught (1709—1792)

Bound in a chain of women, I
sometimes reach out with alarm,
and catch, sometimes, an old reply.

My chain connects me to the farm
that formed your ground, that fed your sheep.
The chain is just a Scottish charm,

but you grow frantic if I sleep.
The roots that dig around your tomb
deepen, till I reach to keep

the feel of your low-ceilinged room,
the branches that burst from your broom.

Calendars

A poem in chants for four voices:

Chorus
Persephone
Demeter
Hades

In the winding
of the vine
our voices stretch
from us and twine —

No, going into the waiting places
is not easy. Flowers fade there.

around the year's
fermented wine —

Mostly, it's surrender of wanting,
or the fear that a flame will be dampened—
or that everything warm will come rushing
over me with reproach—or that endless

needles could be ranged in the tunnel—
or that my bare feet would be slippery—

Yellow. Fall roars
down to the ground,
loud, in the leafy sun that pours
liquid through doors.
Yellow, the leaves go down

or that once I'm down in that darkness
someone outside will block off the entrance—

Touches of gold stipple the branches,
promising weeks of time —

Thread with Me

My lover, when you riddle with me—

reddening slowly, then suddenly free,
turned like a key

Oh! the falling flowers have caught me
by dipping yellow, purple towards the hunger—

—the hard, the intricate dark
(I hear the notes of your words
ring for me cool as the birds,

my lover—

through the long year's
fermenting wine

her thin stems turning, held to be—lost—

my lover, when you thread with me

Now you are uncurled and cover our eyes
with the edge of winter sky,
leaning over us in icy stars

through this night- shot

night- shot dark

is never easy.

Flowers fade here.

Voices pull me on through the cavern
from the new season. Her voice old, silent—

our hands, our breasts, our curves
curl through our hands and ravel—

On damp limestone, a violet curling—

my lover, when you riddle with me
the hard, the intricate dark.

Rack me with courage, spring,
come kill me, flowers;

if we are shadows, come;

make me our shadows

as I reach for flowers.

Desire for Quiet

Silence may lead deep and make me mad.
If I say "water," it might answer "mud."

The quietness might stop and make me sad,
And kill my carp, my colors' golden blood.

Why should I dig a place for it, here where
The dark is dry grass tipped by brutal flowers?

Lammas Chant

August 1

(two voices, alternating)

Fill the earth's belly full.

Fill the earth's belly full.
Bring the food, bring the grain.
There are cold months ahead
Give them peace in the ground.

Bring the food, bring the grain.

Fill the earth's belly full.
bring the food, bring the grain.
There are cold months ahead.
Give them peace in the ground.

There are cold months ahead.
Give them peace in the ground.

Fill the earth's belly full;
bring the food, bring the grain.
There are cold months ahead.
Give them peace in the ground.

A Dance for the Inland Sea

Water that moves, in a bodylike stream,
through its cool channels fills the warm prairie's dream.
Waking to tend it, the grass-moving sky

pours with grasses. Big Bluestem's drinking roots lie
nine feet down the waving, remembering sod
they have swum through, to feed on, to build. When it swings
like a wing in small flight, when it sways,
turkey feet murmur, red three-toed feet sing.

Little Bluestem, as copper as autumn or clay,
floating seeds past the prairie's dense, watery hand
till they shimmer to columns, wet smoke on the land;

Indian Grass, lapping up the spattering sun;
prairies step slower than palaces, down
under the teeming roof of the ground,
quiet as animals. Then, when they rise,
prairies, like palaces, loom, and surprise.

No Snake

Inside my Eden I can find no snake.
There's not one I could look to and believe,
obey and then be ruined by and leave
because of, bearing children and an ache.

I circle down on Eden from above,
searching the fields in solitude and love
like a high hawk. He would never forsake

this place that's made again of memory;
he'd wait in that tree below me, spring
out towards my growing shadow, let it bring
a sudden hope that he could coil free;

but he's not here. Only mountains that curve,
and dip around the valley when I swerve,
settle with dark heights, as I near the tree.

Coy Mistress

Sir, I am not a bird of prey:
a Lady does not seize the day.
I trust that brief Time will unfold
our youth, before he makes us old.
How could we two write lines of rhyme
were we not fond of numbered Time
and grateful to the vast and sweet
trials his days will make us meet?
The Grave's not just the body's curse;
no skeleton can pen a verse!
So while this numbered World we see,
let's sweeten Time with poetry,
and Time, in turn, may sweeten Love
and give us time our love to prove.
You've praised my eyes, forehead, breast:
you've all our lives to praise the rest.

Frost's Grave

I think of your quiet grave now and again
When hope or fear has rolled me out of sleep
Close to my husband's side, to lean again
Against his breathing human side, to keep
Myself breathed in his liquid human breath.
I think of your nurturing grave, because your death
Has made you a place I like to imagine going:
Opening the gate to your grave, entering in,
Reaping your silence where a small tree, growing
Generous in the forgiveness of your sin,
Leans over your stone, the grass, your bones, the grass,
The grass. The grass. I like to imagine frost there, hung
Like frost on a beach in November, when the sun
Rises on winter, just as it rose on spring,
On the humid decision to grow, past everything.

A Seed for Spring Equinox

March 21

. . . till I feel the earth around the place my head has lain
under winter's touch, and it crumbles. Slanted weight of clouds.
Reaching with my head and shoulders past the open crust

dried by spring wind. Sun. Tucking through the ground
that has planted cold inside me, made its waiting be my food.
Now I watch the watching dark my light's long-grown dark
makes known.

Hostage Wildflowers

Daisy-grouped hanging sea, wet paintbrush filled
with devil-drops, purple vetch steering its barge,
soaked as long-cold sea-houses, and less tame:

close visitors, the gentle places in grass came
to earth. They trap you wild while the large
rain centers and your drops fall, build, fall, build.

Thanksgiving

for Julian

Earth is getting ready to harden and dim
in an unmoving winter. A dry yellow curl
bends the grasses the long year has tufted and brimmed.

Their tops start to flatten, hushed by the hurl
the wind sends through the trees, and soon they will bow.
Layered on grain, quick-shadowed like pearl,

sky-thick gray clouds anchor down to plow
the black plunging earth. As the furrows grow strange
and dark with their shadows, the morning grows. How

can a harvest this cold wrinkle open and change?
Laced into earth by their last anxious stalks,
the fields wait. Nothing's there, in the sky's empty range,

but the emptying wind that listens and talks,
or else barely stutters, stumbling by
on its way to bring snow. The day-darkened hawks

slow their long wheeling, up the thin sky,
and then push back downward with shuddering grace.
Is this the dry answer that time makes? The high

piled grain, the bleached houses and barns, lean. You place
fourteen dense kernels of looming seed-corn
with care in my left hand. Their saffron-hard trace
of the sun is alive, a long memory torn
from a stalk. So smooth, they call quiet, as loud
as your opened eyes spoke the first day you were born.

Gulf War and Child: A Curse

He is sleeping, his fingers curled,
his belly pooled open, his legs gathered, still
in their bent blossom victory.

I couldn't speak of "war" (though we all do),
if I were still the woman who gave birth
to this soft-footed one: his empty hand,
his calling heart, that border of new clues.

May the hard birth our two heartbeats unfurled
for two nights that lasted as long as this war
make all sands rage, until the mouth of war
drops its cup, this bleeding gift we poured.

Walk With Me

Walk with me just a while, body of sunlight,
body of grass, surface of trees,
head bending to the earth we have tasted,
body of death, surface of leaves.
Sinking hooves in the mud by the river,
root of the live earth, live through my body.
Sinking body, walk in me now.

Four
WATER

Edge, Atlantic, July

I picked my way nearer along the shocking rock shelf,
hoping the spray would rise up to meet me, myself.

Seagulls roared louder and closer than anything planned;
I looked out to see and forgot I could still see the land.

Lost in a foaming green crawl, I grew smaller than me;
shrunk in a tidepool, I heaved, and I wondered. The sea

grew like monuments for me. Each wave and its coloring shadow,
bereft, wild and laden with wrack, spoke for me and had no

need of my words anymore. I was open and glad
at last, grateful like seaweed and glad, since I had

no place on the rocks but a voice, and the voice was the sea's:
not my own. Just the sea's.

A Carol for Carolyn

"It is easy to be a poet, / brim with transparent water."
—Carolyn Kizer, "In the First Stanza"

I dreamed of a poet who gave me a whale
that shadowed clear pools through the kelp-making shade.
When beached sea-foam dried on the rocks, it would sail
down currents that gathered to pool and cascade
with turbulent order.
She brims with transparent water,
as mother and poet and daughter.

The surface is broken and arching and full,
impelled by the passions of nation and woman.
The waves build and fall; the deep currents pull
toward rocky pools cupping the salt of the human.
The ocean she's authored
brims, with transparent water,
for poet and mother and daughter.

On the Wide Sand

There is a surge
that comes to me
as with a welcome
tirelessly

and fills my waiting
with a curve
spilling reflections
from above

till cloud and current
air and land
rocks and sparkles
understand

that the movement
of a tide
is as quiet
as a wing,

wafting open
to ride
on the spur
of everything.

Over Dark Arches

Naked and thin and wet as if with rain,
bursting I come out of somewhere, bursting again.
And like a great building that breathes under sunlight
over dark arches, your body is there,

And my milk moves under your tongue—

where currents from earth linger under cool stone
rising to me and my mouth makes a circle
over your silence

You reach through your mouth to find me—

Bursting out of your body that held me for years,
as the rain wets the earth with its bodies—

And my thoughts are milk to feed you

till we turn and are empty,

till we turn and are full.

The Task

A voice and the same voice, older

Sometimes at night,
And every day,
I dip my buckets in the spring house.
Its roof is moss, and grows.

I miss the dark knowledge
Of the taste of that water.
I've forgotten the softness
Of that wet wood

Let the door toss to.
Kneel by the drip of a beam.
Be low in th forest. Look out.
Be needle height to pines.
Now grow your arms —

But from this still
Present time
I still see her
Who knew the taste —

Now, with my buckets dipped,
I carry or balance
Or brim
Or whatever you'd like to call it, old woman,
My buckets back home
By this path.

The Woman on the Beach

for Wallace Stevens

She could cliff and order waves, if they were climb-
ing up to reach her touch, or curling in
with drowning, freezing, fingers. . . She hears

the phantoms tooling over shale, their long
unrooting waverings singing the air
into her hands. Then, as she plants and pours,
learning her music, with no difference how

she seeds them out, or harvests in, or racks
the dark with her questioning, she pulls the caves
from sleep with her answering chant and noticing shore.
The waves won't hear her now; she won't feed them;

and it won't matter how she pulls them in,
gathers their green in seedlings weighted all
spiralling through, to make her bounded dream.

Watching the Whale

A hard gray wave, her fin, walks out on the water
that thickens to open and then parts open, around her.

Measured by her delved water, I follow her fill
into and out of green light in the depth she has spun

through the twenty-six fathoms of her silent orison,
then sink with her till she rises, lulled with the krill.

Beads of salt spray stop me, like metal crying.
Her cupped face breathes its spouts, like a jewel-wet prong.

In a cormorant's barnacle path, I trail her, spun
down through my life in the making of her difference,

fixing my mouth, with the offerings of silence,
on her dark whale-road where all green partings run,

where ocean's hidden bodies twist fathoms around her,
making her green-fed hunger grow fertile as water.

Isthmus

As deep as green can make it go,
As gold as it can stay,
As many holes as breathe the sand—
As webbed as Ripples—stray—

As simple as the sunset looms
As close—or far—as land—-
As strong as seaweed floating— home—
I love—the Water's hand.

Love Leaves the Tides

Courtship is pulling with your full-moon heart
to bring out patterns. Patterns dry, crisp tides
that crescent up the beach, past sifted sand,
as sunset comes. When all the shores are dark,

night pulls with courtship's tides (Love leaves the tides
aside, to push on further up the sand,
to change far pools, to ebb into the heart
of earth and leave it salty, full, and dark).

Rain Birth

This is the rainy season, like a birth
around our windows. In your open eyes,
and in the heart whose hands, beating inside
my hands, have opened out, we meet the rain.
The quiet sentinels—the trees—unfold
outside the window. Light and cold
go running through the day. In the full tide
that loosens skies to water, in the sea
that comes to find me, now I see your eyes,
and, perishing from salt, I dry my eyes.

The Last Mermother

It started with a tentative tug, a touch confined
without a glance or the pressure of a hand.
Then it teased me like a simple, other mind
across my own, vibrating with command.
Then I almost fell, as she charged high, and fanned
open her tailfins, arching through the spray
of her own raging white wake. Don't look away;

Listen! I breathed, and she tore away the line,
and showed me her face—those empty eyes—beside
the dock. She howled, stretching her hand to mine,
floating her tail in the rocking of the tide
as she clung to the slippery post below. I tried
to look at her and saw that it was true.
What would you have done? I helped her through

the railing. Draped with clammy seaweed strands,
she wiggled her huge shoulders down and lay
flopping along the pier, with her open hands
still held towards me. Now I know that was the day
I lost my mind. She's followed me the way
a beggar could haunt a doorway. She's in my shade
whenever I feel empty or afraid.

Look at her now; by now she's growing old.
We hear her every night, that singing, through
the heartless air, carried on the cold
enchantment of the California dew,
futile and endless notes, a wordless clue
poured out over the deafened land. I wish,
sometimes, I'd thrown her back in like a fish,

when I saw her breasts. A mother! I still can't say

if my fishing hook killed it, or if she
dropped it in the struggle, but of course it died that day.
And I know wherever it fell, there must be
a shrinking in the waves, the hissing sea,
a crust of sand still thickening on the edge
of its quiet bones.

Blossom of the Salt

When ocean
pulls towards ocean,
leaving seaweed
on the rocks,

it will dry
to curl outward
with the blossom
of the salt.

Peace and Ice

The quiet island is still there,
Although I came away
From peace and left the moment bare
To fester, and to fray.

But peace is there, because the ice
Piles in the tiny cove
to find the white reflections lace
Of clouds, and waves, and love.

Dusk Song

Over the big bed in the small room
The flat shadow
Turned, thinning our walls
Insistently,
Turning and turning us closer and closer to salt wind
In from the sea.

I could sing a song about a long-gone lover,
Cape Cod dusk, Cape Cod shadow;
I sang a song then about the Cape Cod shadow,
Over door and wall, over
Shoulder and shoulder.

Did I have a face and did it lie
In shadow
Turning and turning your glances away?

Once there was a song about the Cape Cod shadow;
I sang the song.
The flat shadow turned over our walls and brought the sea in.
The song kept turning.

Landing under Water, I see Roots

All the things we hide in water
hoping we won't see them go—
(forests growing under water
press against the ones we know)—

and they might have gone on growing
and they might now breathe above
everything I speak of sowing
(everything I try to love).

Whales Who Keep the Past

The great past has gray keepers
forming arches far away—

wild leapers, gray archers.
Words they keep cold stay.

Name

Spring Grove Cemetery, Cincinnati

Brown-gold with bronze water, broken in blossom,
they shake as you shine over swans, your wedged bodies
pushing the sky towards the monumented island
where long generations of geese flew before you.

Long generations of geese flew before you,
sang out, and melted over the graves.
Won't long cries of feathers pile a moment
close on another? Isn't there one name?

Close on another, isn't there one name?
Mourning I ask you, oh, mourning I ask you;
so went the questions the geese did not answer;
is this voice a music you mourn with, each time;

Is this voice a music you mourn with, each time?
When questions had asked me, I moved in their bodies
to follow the light on the movement of swans,

to follow the movements of light on the swans.

Pearl

Reaching with eyes, they covered her as a girl,
leaving a grain of gaze, the irritant stare
women must cover everywhere, like pearl.

Even in her own room alone, she curled
back from the windows gleaming with their glare.
Reaching with eyes, they covered her, as a girl,

stopping her gaze with a long look, unfurled,
taking her in as if she belonged there,
a woman covered everywhere, with pearls

draping her throat, before she learned to whirl
beside the mirror, pierce her ears, or twine her hair.
Reaching with eyes, they covered her, as a girl

covers and hunches herself back in, to coil
less of her toward the voyeur. But beware.
Women can cover everything, like pearls

orbed and alive. A living ocean swirls.
We encompass it, and spiral everywhere.
Reaching with eyes, they covered, in the girl,
What the woman covers: everything, like pearl.

A House by the Sea

For my mother Margaret Evelyn Rockwell (Maggie Mer)

I live in a house by the sea
and its boats come up rising to me.

I hear them on their thick swells
casting unending spells

on my own self by the sand,
touching my watery hand.

I live in a house by the shore.
I have nothing left, no more,

and no-one comes to me
but the whisper of the sea.

That is all I need—
That is my kind of seed.

The Seafarer

From the Anglo-Saxon

I keep the track
of a song true of me:
I'll tell of trials,
struggling times,
hard days,
and how I endured.
I have borne
such bitter cares,
held on ships
whole houses of cares.
Awful sea-waves
tossed where I kept
narrowed watches
on the stern at night
and the ship beat cliffs.

Thronged in cold
were my feet,
bound in frost
with chains of cold,
while hunger slit
my ocean-weary mood.
They do not know,
whom fair things
befall on land,
how, care-worn wretch,
I stayed at sea
and wintered an exile's
icy tracks,
shorn of kin,
hung with icicles.
Hail-showers flew.

There I heard only
the whirring sea,
ice-cold wave,
or else the call
of swans for a game,
gannet's laughter
and curlew's song
for human laughter,
mew's singing
for mead to drink.
Storms beat the stone cliffs;
the tern answered,
icy-feathered.
No strong kinfolk
could help the heart
that hollowness held.
They hardly know,
who have life's joy
by staying in towns,
they of few hardships,
lustful and flushed,
how often I, weary,
was forced to stay out
on the salty sea.

Nights' shadow darkened,
ground bound by frost;
coldest corn. . .

a thought in my heart
the high waves,
my heart's need
my spirit out
seeking only
And there is no person
nor so good in gifts,
nor so eager in acts,
that they don't sorrow
about what Heaven
their mind is not
or on joy in love,
or on anything else—
We are always longing,

snow from the north,
hail fell on earth,

And now! there beats
that I should try
the salty tossing;
always urges
away from here
another place.
so bold on the earth,
nor so quick in youth,
nor with friends so kind,
at sea always,
might give to them
on harping, or on rings,
or on bliss in this world,
but on that tossing.
we who move on water. . .

Beach of Edges

A drift of snow edges a new drift of sand
As edges grow deeper. It's March, month of edges.
Wet rocks yield to pebbles like opening hands.

The glisten of rockweed trails, splutters, and bends,
And sparkles of rivulets bounce down in ledges.
A drift of snow edges a new drift of sand;

It's March, month of edges, and I'm left to stand
Alone outside time as new light pulls and nudges
Wet rocks. Yield to pebbles like opening hands,

Light; pull me from winter. How have I planned
For light that's not winter, for live light that fledges
A drift of snow, edges a new drift of sand

Beyond my last sight, and waves me like a wand
Out back over the surges of these rocking sedges?
Wet rocks yield to pebbles like opening hands—

I want to go back to him, as to the land.
Light, carry me over from the wild old grudges!
A drift of snow edges a new drift of sand.
Wet rocks yield to pebbles, like opening hands.

Tarot: the Magician Card

Rain wets the wand, wind moves a sword,
lightening lights crystal where the thundering cup
forms me a channel and takes on a word,
pouring the pentacle I gather up.
Time carves the storm in the palm of my hand,
till it fills with shapes that send me down
through my river-body. Do I stand
at a table the waiting planet surrounds?
Through my own fingers, eyes, and palm,
and through other worlds, huge or small,
one fury spins and turns me calm;
I breathe and watch it land and fall,
holding what I hardly know or see,
filled with the storm that makes, makes me.

Oil Spill

I was angry at our mother,
I was blanketed in shame,
And I tried to call out to her,
And I tried to hear my name
In her silences and shadow,
In the patience of her heart,

But I only found the ugliness,
And now the ruptures start.
Oil, oil, oil, oil,
Burning without ash:
I was angry at my planet
And I smothered it with trash.

Oil, oil, oil, oil,
Roiling brown and slow
Through the womb of our mother.
No.
No.
No.

The Bass

Casting along the sand after the fish,
you ran, aiming to club a great blue-
fish at the water's edge;
then, ankles in salt, gaffed a bass,
late in the day, ran the shore,
drove home in a pick-up, scaled it, went in, and shut the door.

I might have come and hung around your screen door
while the moon came out, and you ate your fish
in kitchen light lying against the blue
blacking night, with your humming a sound the deep bass
of the ocean thickened at the still sand's edge,

as it pounded salty at the sand's edge,
sending cold and fish and rhythm to your door,
calling its melodies of mackerel and bass,
flounder and cod, skate, goosefish, dogfish,
halibut, swordfish, shark, eel, blue-
fish, calling you to come back out to shore;
then I might have seen you come back out to shore,

walking with your jacket to the sea's edge
to look at the noisy black smell of gray-blue
gone dark, and at seaweed in the dark, and back at your yellow
door,
and to remember the taste of fish, to think of the taste of fish,
and of salt, and of clubbing and gaffing the bass.

It took you a long afternoon to find the bass,
club it, gaff it, and drag to the shore
the flopping, eyed, scaled, wet stabbed silver fish,
sandy with its dragging from the ocean's edge.
When you put it in the pick-up in the wind and shut the door,

it was colder, the sky and waves were darkening from blue,

And you thought of home in the darkening blue,
home, corn, chowder—and the bass
spiced by the sea coming in the screen door,
warmed by the cold wind blowing from shore,
at night, with cold noise at the edge,
and out from the edge, ocean blind, full of fish

that swim black, blue, cold, far from shore;
halibut, cod, far from the edge
of your door, where you watched the waves.

Five

MATRIX

This Land

As I went walking in the land of our heart,
I found the animals crying.
Their mouths and warm bodies were sudden and slow
And they moved slow and hard to the edge of the woods.
Their legs and their heartbeats and skins were dying.
They curled up like snails at the end of the world.

"This land is your land, this land is my land."

As I went out walking, the trees became bark.
They turned in their power and knowledge and pain.
Their arms grew wide open, their lives fell apart.
I heard them in peace and I heard them in horror,
And each leaf or hand was the eye of a world.

"This land is your land, this land is my land."

As I went walking by the side of the sea,
I found the waves understanding.
They rolled out of silence and into the mist,
And into the light where it seemed they were pouring.
They roiled with pollution and anger and love,
And the currents of freedom kept rolling.

"This land is your land, this land is my land."

Interpenetrate

Like the bleached fibers and their haunted ink,
interpenetrate each other's solitudes,

not penetrating, not dissolving; stay
rolled with the single patterns of the days,

linking through pages to burn with speaking lace
and thread to bodies, evenly alive.

Spells

From music, I bore
Some gold-stone fins,
but they sank away
through the waffled shallows.

From nature, I gleaned
Some hope of rice—
But it edged deep away
In sunk stone bowls.

So then I asked
For bowls and fins;
I asked for a hand
that could gather them back

into finning the shallows,
gilding, rounding.
I guessed me a hand
That could gather bowls open.

When I had asked
Whom I had guessed,
She sent my asking out.

Now over and over
she sends it back.
Over and over it answers me.
Over and over it answers, as she gives it,

in the speech of fins, and in the speech of bowls.

Rhiannon

A child is ranging, like a young horse;
a child is growing, like a gray mare.
She carries the coastal wind in her teeth
and the furious sun in her mane.

Spider Woman

Your thoughts in a web have covered the sky.
A thread from the northwest is carrying beads from the rain,
a thread from the southwest is carrying beads from the rain,
a thread from the southeast carries bright beads,
a thread from the northeast is bringing the beads
of the rain that has filled up the sky.
Spider, you have woven a chain
stretching with rain over the sky.

Inanna

A young goddess, full of love, fresh with the touch of a husband,
carrying power and rich with anger, strength, urgency, understanding,
follows the direction her ear has led her, down to the place where the
underworld glistens.

At each door she removes a jewel, a belt, a ceremonial robe.
At each door, she is less and more. She bows down through the seventh door.

The young goddess is dead, and waiting. The young goddess is dead.
A goddess goes down, and I can see her. She needs to go, decides to go.
A goddess goes down, and I can hear her.

Coatlique

She listens for breathing
around her in the night.
Below the mountain,
families are sleeping.
When will she wake
to bring the morning?
When will she birth
sun and stars?
When will her mist
give birth to the moon?

The skulls are breathing,
as quiet in her necklace
as darkness will keep them.

Brigid

Ring, ring, ring, ring! Hammers fall.
Your gold will all be beaten
over sudden flaming fire
moving from you, the pyre. Sweeten
your cauldron, until the sun
runs with one flame through the day
and the healing water will sing,
linger on tongues, burn away.

Nut

I cry for my lost days, I cry for my childhood,
I cry for the goddess coming down from the sky.
I cry for a place on the ground for my feet
and I call for a place on the ground for my hands.
In the daylight my hands reach out for home;
in the night, the stars connect the stones
and find their way. The shooting stars
fall from your breasts, your arms.

Aphrodite

Aphrodite, come to me,
even while I lie resting with my infant.
Cover me with your sweet certainty.

Changing Woman

If we change as she is changing,
if she changes as we change

(If she changes, I am changing)

Who is changing, as I bend
down to what the sky has sent us?

(Is she changing, or the same?)

Eve

When mother Eve took the first apple down
from the tree that grew where nature's heart had been
and came tumbling, circling, rosy, into sin,
which goddesses were lost, and which were found?
What spirals moved in pity and unwound
across our mother's body with the spin
of planets lost for us and all her kin?
What serpents curved their mouths into a frown,
but left their bodies twined in us like threads
that lead us back to her? Her presence warms,
and if I follow closely through the maze,
it is to where her remembered reaching spreads
in branching gifts, it is to her reaching arms
that I reach, as if for something near to praise.

Kali

I walked cautiously, knowing my belly
full of wide wings, night, and starlight.

The dark highway led me from the others,
and then a narrow path led to Kali.
I could see her, sitting, sewing
on a huge tapestry as rich as blood.

I walked cautiously, knowing my belly
full of wide wings, night, and starlight.

I saw in its folds a glimpse of creation,
animals, planets, mountains, and trees,
embroidered thick with contrasts and colors,
on a background as warm as blood.

I walked cautiously, knowing my belly
full of wide wings, night, and starlight.

Did I have to explain what I wanted?
Did she wait till I tried to explain?
No, of course not; she'd known my story
before I had come. She was Kali.

I walked cautiously, knowing my belly
full of wide wings, night, and starlight.

Letter for Emily Dickinson

When I cut words you never may have said
into fresh patterns, pierced in place with pins,
ready to hold them down with my own thread,
they change and twist sometimes, their color spins
loose, and your spider generosity
lends them from language that will never be
free of you after all. My sampler reads,
"called back." It says, "she scribbled out these screeds."
It calls, "she left this trace, and now we start"—
in stitched directions that follow the leads
I take from you, as you take me apart.

You wrote some of your lines while baking bread,
propping a sheet of paper by the bins
of salt and flour, so if your kneading led
to words, you'd tether them as if in thin
black loops on paper. When they sang to be free,
you captured those quick birds relentlessly
and kept a slow, sure mercy in your deeds,
leaving them room to peck and hunt their seeds
in the white cages your vast iron art
had made by moving books, and lives, and creeds.
I take from you as you take me apart.

Tribute

"You'll find--it when you try to die--"
— Emily Dickinson

When there are no words left to live,
I have elected hers

to haunt me till the margins give
and I am left alone.

One voice has vanished through my own
To make me like a stone,

one that the falling leaves will stay
not over, but upon.

Goddess

There is no spoken sentence. All she says
will stay. It will be quiet when I go
out of the room and stop being a priestess.
She looks down. Her quiet death is unashamed,
undimming power like receding grain
that waves inside my heart in shocking rag-
ing silence, beating in the window light.
She will not go to make new presences,
but stays to go. Her presence is the loss.
In the cold sky that waits each season out,
her body's ancient stars make restless calls
against the throne that quivers in my heart
as fiercely in love as in the hate
on which four thousand years of sorrow fed.
Her birdsong joys shine ruins in my heart.
I seem to stand on some undying plain,
watching the monuments that dawn again.
The gravity of goddess is above
my eyes, though never gone from history.
So many must have noticed, with this shock,
such patient looking up, and looking down.

Elegy for my Father

HLF, August 8, 1918—August 22, 1997

"Bequeath us to no earthly shore until
Is answered in the vortex of our grave
The seal's wide spindrift gaze towards paradise."
—**Hart Crane,** "Voyages"

"If a lion could talk, we couldn't understand it"
—**Ludwig Wittgenstein**

Under the ocean that stretches out wordlessly
past the long edge of the last human shore,
there are deep windows the waves haven't opened,
where night is reflected through decades of glass.
There is the nursery, there is the nanny,
there are my father's unreachable eyes
turned towards the window. Is the child uneasy?
His is the death that is circling the stars.

In the deep room where candles burn soundlessly
and peace pours at last through the cells of our bodies,
three of us are watching, one of us is staring
with the wide gaze of a wild, wave-fed seal.
Incense and sage speak in smoke loud as waves,
and crickets sing sand towards the edge of the hourglass.
We wait outside time, while night collects courage
around us. The vigil is wordless. And you

watch the longest, move the farthest, besieged by your breath,
pulling into your body. You stare towards your death,
head arched on the pillow, your left fingers curled.
Your mouth sucking gently, unmoved by these hours
and their vigil of salt spray, you show us how far
you are going, and how long the long minutes are,
while spiralling night watches over the room
and takes you, until you watch us in turn.
Lions speak their own language. You are still breathing.

Here is release. Here is your pillow,
cool like a handkerchief pressed in a pocket.
Here is your white tousled long growing hair.
Here is a kiss on your temple to hold you
safe through your solitude's long steady war;
here, you can go. We will stay with you,
keeping the silence we all came here for.

Night, take his left hand, turning the pages.
Spin with the windows and doors that he mended.
Spin with his answers, patient, impatient.
Spin with his dry independence, his arms
warmed by the needs of his family, his hands
flying under the wide, carved gold ring, and the pages
flying so his thought could fly. His breath slows,
lending its edges out to the night.

Here is his open mouth. Silence is here
like one more new question that he will not answer.
A leaf is his temple. The dark is the prayer.
He has given his body; his hand lies above
the sheets in a symbol of wholeness, a curve
of thumb and forefinger, ringed with wide gold,
and the instant that empties his breath is a flame
faced with a sudden cathedral's new stone.

Another Reluctance

Chestnuts fell in the charred season,
fell finally, finding room
in air to open their old cases
so they gleam out from the gold leaves
in dust now, where they dropped down.

I watch them, waiting for winter,
husks open and holding on.
Their rusted rims are rigid-hard
but cling soft to the clear brown.
This low light sinks soon

from the old tree in the only sun,
from the gifts that have fallen. Cold children's
chestnuts, hidden in small caches,
have gone hollow, with gleams gone,
grain gone, now the children are home.

Samhain

October 31

In the season leaves should love,
since it gives them leave to move
through the wind, towards the ground
they were watching while they hung,
legend says there is a seam
stitching darkness like a name.

Now when dying grasses veil
earth from the sky in one last pale
wave, as autumn dies to bring
winter back, and then the spring,
we who die ourselves can peel
back another kind of veil

that hangs among us like thick smoke.
Tonight at last I feel it shake.
I feel the nights stretching away
thousands long behind the days,
till they reach the darkness where
all of me is ancestor.

I turn my hand and feel a touch
move with me, and when I brush
my young mind across another,
I have met my mother's mother.
Sure as footsteps in my waiting
self, I find her, and she brings

arms that hold answers for me,
intimate, waiting, bounty:
"Carry me." She leaves this trail
through a shudder of the veil,
and leaves, like amber where she stays,
a gift for her perpetual gaze.

The August Porch

One afternoon: I think I like it
better for cut browns
apples
lumber

than evening for the ravelling of slats to emerald.

There's no gleam to the wicker.
Shadows might well
not be cast.

The trees are scanty
with the weight
of apples
they have finished.

But wistaria raises
its inchworm head and hunts
for the walls of this porch.

Something's waiting to run out on us.
The mist
and creak
of wines is due
when we run out of dusk.

Still Life

A sunny afternoon; think of Vermeer.
Here is the apple, here the rounding side
of the blue pitcher. On the scrubbed wood just here,
she puts the pitcher down, so that the slide
of drops against its lip catches what light
there is for pitchers here this afternoon.
She does not really see the drops, or quite
attend the blue. A common thing. But soon
the tide will turn, and salty smells will rise
to circle in the street, and to her ears
will come the voices. Then doorways to her eyes,
then other days than this—afternoons, years.
She will stop to hold this moment near,
and drop the pitcher, and betray Vermeer.

A Fragment of Sappho

It is not appropriate, in a household
Given to the Muses. Those lamentations
Do not belong here.

Keys

Phi Beta Kappa poem, Yale University, 2011

Like an island, a key makes a door. In the surge
Of its mineral clarity, seas come unbound.
Though an arch curves together, the keystone will stay
Braced in gravity, locked by immensity, wound
To a temple in air by the spiraling play
That could tumble much heavier forces. What's found
Past the musical notes that cascade and converge
In a key, past the tock the tick carries away
When it's wound by a key? There are patterns that merge

Meanings, silent until we code them open,
Clued to us by the random knowing tribes:
Carvings, letters, hands, faces, symbols, stars.
Each warm friction's vibration circumscribes
One more seat in the clearing where we are
Gathered, circling a home we can't describe.
What's the word but a word that can't be spoken?
Who'd tear pleasure out past life's iron bars?
Where's the use of a code that won't be broken?

A ring of keys hangs like a question at your side.
You move through the answering darkness like a key,
While windows of moonlight branch down the catacombs
And rustle each prisoner into mystery.
Each lock, like each room, is alone till the opening comes;
Your ring reaches one, then another. Liberty
Repeats down the corridor, doors pulled open wide,
Exploding more showers of sweetness through the combs
Whose locks had been waiting for one key to be tried.

A Crown of Flowers for Beltane

May 1

May is here, come around,
Find a place on the ground.

Find a place on the ground,
and the flowers rain down.

And the flowers rain down.
We are gorgeous today.

We are gorgeous today,
We're alive for the May.

We're alive for the May,
May is here. Come around.

A Wedding on Earth

That all the woods may answer, and your eccho ring.
—Edmund Spenser

Love's feet keep us ready to dance the ground,
rooting deep with steps there is time to hear;
love's leaves carry spiral sun's gift-light down
full-tipped blossoms that fruit to reappear.
Petal, stamen, pistil —all fragrant dust
sings with that pollen lust.
May your wedding day fly your pollen hearts
earthward, home again. May your marriage share
leafing's, budding's, blossoming's wildest arts,
married home in bodies that come to dare
bend, to our planet's care.

Marriage is a field where the Earth's sweet skin
stretches, waking open through fertile seeds.
Rhythms love has made to grow new begin.
Shadowed seed-time's soul-sweet unfurling leads
time-fed opposites, soaked with endless night,
to trust each others' height.
(May earth make you follow Her steady songs,
sounding ways your marriage, compassion's tool,
generous bringer of joy's right-gathering wrongs,
simple puzzle, tangling oldest rule,
moves through each molecule.)

Out there in the cold deepest far black holes
(emptiest solid reach of oldest space
where new stars and solitude grow), strong souls
shimmer open thickly as time. They trace
gifting dark, charming changes through the same,
ringing love's ever-name.
Bring your waiting souls there together. Ring

warmth from coolness, coolness from what is full,
home from your nights, till those longest echoes ring
again. Hear, feel, how each lunging particle
rocks with its surging lull:

deep where long-held faith in our silent guides
flows, like minerals, into love's secret folds,
hear how Earth and heat midwife crystal tides,
strengthening the shapes listening patterns hold.
Build, remember, and love, as your energy
bursts with polarity.
Forge! Come together in fire and in Earth,
willing difference out of the ground you change,
meeting powers, until your meetings' birth—
constant metamorphoses rearranged —
grows, both the same — and strange.

Oceans, deserts, forests and rivers move
with the spinning bodies, sounding hearts,
surfacing eyes, and searching wings of love
till the one and many, and whole and parts,
touch and blend, to marry in their own time,
ringing with moving's rhyme.
Universes spiral and climates clear
in the linking spaces such love exhales.
Grow yourselves with the passions that twine love near,
voicing, dancing desire's fountain trails,
humming with ancient scales.

Let your bodies make a body of bodies—cool
with sweet spaces anchored by love's vast charm,
answers quickened to beat and roll and spool
with the pores of a question, rich and warm
where pools of kiss and hope and remembering meet,
crossed in their sculpting heat.

Then enter, enter the language of your skins
where motion mentions silence, and words spill light
out through actual air, till pooled touch begins
the spin of separate souls towards one wondered flight
and one, believed, delight.

Feel yourselves how those herons, eagles, swallows,
cardinals, doves and finches, sparrows, terns,
raise on long-held wings through a surge that follows,
dips, falls, surges, then wills back up and learns
love's warm mornings, sung like brief songs from trees
(forests darkening to ease).
As each fruit that drips down Earth's Goddess chin
spills its sugar over Her ancient face,
feel your seeds, which vibrate alive within
each day's hardened pod. Pull each lost embrace
from its last hiding place,

tuned and ready. Ready, now! Welcome love,
salt and sweet, till it spirals through your hands,
warms and tingles, calls back the memories of
truest lives. Give them back to Earth and stand
here together, claiming the way love feels
newborn on land that heals.
Feel how moose, fox, crocodile, koala bear,
cheetah, elephant, mouse, deer, lion, squirrel
cry with single breaths until they may pair,
ears and mouths poured open as bodies skirl
towards the enspiralled whirl,

and then reach, through the meanings humans need
one more mind to touch with, the timeless pairs—
uncornered circling, circling circles' lairs—
intersection of triangles and squares,
long paradoxes, shaped in geometry's

aisled community.
Goddess of living weddings, may this pair
pair with abundance and curl, wide and alive,
through each leaf they'll send through the long beauty.
Grow them in the roots and the blooms that thrive.
Harvest them as they strive.

Marriage is the mirror and crucible
where a true plain face turns to see its own
fullness empty, its emptiness made full
in the shadows that blended love and bone,
half-invisible, burned clear by the light,
cast under mutual sight.
May the path of this wedding guide your strengths
under your weaving promises to go
into new realms of kinship, through the lengths
of the days that move you, so fast, so slow,
from everything you know.

May hope turns towards peace in your valleyed cove,
as love learns new flights, and new kinds of birth,
sacred spouses. Share marriage. Claim your love
in the sight of these people and this earth.
Touch your hands. Touch words. Touching here now, touch
all with your happiness—
earth, time, family, friends, and this naked day.
Bless your hearts that have listened for every test —
wanted, needed, all blessings love can say —
strong to hold your silences, find your rest —
wise, to believe love best.

Acknowledgments

"The Task" was composed in 1975 and is published here for the first time.

"On the Wide Sand" was first published in *Pratik*.

"Mbote, Kinshasa" was first published in *Capitals*, edited by Abhay K (Bloomsbury, 2016).

"The Bass" was published in West Branch (U.S.), in *Ars Interpres* (Sweden), and in *Obsession: Sestinas in the Twenty-First Century*, ed. Carolyn Beard Whitlow and Marilyn Krysl, Dartmouth College Press, 2013.

"Kali" is excerpted and adapted from *Among the Goddesses: An Epic Libretto in Seven Dreams* (Red Hen Press, 2010).

"A House by the Sea," "Edge, Atlantic, July," "Isthmus," and "Peace and Ice" were first collected in *The Voice Was the Sea: Poems from the Coast of Maine* (Voices from the American Land Series, 2012).

"A Fragment of Sappho," "A Way to See," "Architecture," "Beach of Edges," "Blessing for the Poets," "Earth Day," "First Poem," "Frost's Grave," "Goddess," "Homebirth," "Keys," "List," "Nightmare," "Now in November," "Revelry," "The Seafarer, " "Song of the Sorry Side," "Speak Softly," "Spells," "Tarot: The Magician Card," "When Daphne Ran," and "Your Land" were first collected in *Spells: New and Selected Poems* (Wesleyan University Press, 2013).

"Ancestor," "Another Reluctance," "Aphrodite," "Being a Constellation," "Brigid," "Changing Woman," "Coatlique," "Courtship," "Coy Mistress," "Desire for Quiet," "Encounter," "Eve," "Forest Falling," "Frozen In," "Gulf War and Child," "Hostage Wildflowers," "In Cities," "Inanna," "Insect," "Inside the Violet," "Love Leaves the Tides," "Lucid Waking," "My Raptor," "No Snake," "Nut," "Pearl," "Rain Birth," "Rhiannon," "Running in Church," "Samhain," "Sapphics for Patience." "Spider Woman," "Still Life," "Strangers," "Thanksgiving," "The Circled Sand," "The Door," "The Garden," "The Last Mermother," "The Wish for Eyes," "Three Generations of Secrets" "To the African Violets," "Tribute," "Walk With Me," "Westminster," and "Zaraf's Star" were first collected in *Eve* (Story Line Press, 1997, Reprinted by Carnegie Mellon University Press Contemporary Classics Poetry Series, 2011).

"A Carol for Carolyn," "A Crown of Flowers For Beltane," "A Crown of Leaves for Moneta," "A Dance for the Inland Sea," "A Seed for Spring Equinox," "A Valentine for Hands," "A Wedding on Earth," "Belly," "Blossom of the Salt," "Blue Willow," "Butterfly Lullaby," "Calendars," Caribou Kitchen," "Chain of Women," "Churching," "Conversation,""Earth Goddess and Sky God," "Elegy for My Father," "Final Autumn," "Imbolc Chant," "Interpenetrate," "Iowa Barn," "Lamia to Lycius," "Lammas Chant," "Landing Under Water," "Letter for Emily Dickinson," "Meeting Mammoth Cave," "Menstrual Hut," "Moon," "Mowing," "Name," "Over Dark Arches,""Paravaledellentine," "Summer Solstice Chant," "The August Porch," "The Coming Mirrors," "The Intellect of Woman," "The Woman on the Beach," "Two Bodies,' "Watching the Oregon Whale," "Whales Who Keep the Past," "Wild Yeasts," "Winter Solstice Chant," and "Without a Bird" were first collected in *Calendars* (Tupelo Press, 2003, second edition with CD, 2008).

Index of First Lines

Books by Annie Finch

Books of Poetry

Earth Days (2024)
Spells: New and Selected Poems (2013)
Among the Goddesses (2010)
Calendars (2003)
Eve (1997)
The Encyclopedia of Scotland (1983, 2010

Poetry Chapbooks

The Poetry Witch Little Book of Spells (2019)
Goddess Poems (2016)
The Voice Was the Sea (2012)
Shadow-Bird (2009)
Annie Finch's Greatest Hits (2007)
Home-Birth (2004)
Season Poems (2002)
Catching the Mermother (1996)
The Encyclopedia of Scotland (1982)

Translation

Complete Poetry of Louise Labé (2006)

Poetics

A Poet's Ear: A Handbook of Meter and Form (2013)
A Poet's Craft: A Comprehensive Guide to Making and Sharing Your Poetry (2012)
The Body of Poetry: Essays on Women, Form, and the Poetic Self (2005)
The Ghost of Meter: Culture and Prosody in American Free Verse (1993)

Edited Books

Choice Words: Writers on Abortion (2020)
Measure for Measure: An Anthology of Poetic Meters, with Alexandra Oliver (2015)
Villanelles, with Marie-Elizabeth Mali (2012)
Multiformalisms: Postmodern Poetics of Form, with Susan B. Schultz (2009)
An Exaltation of Forms: Contemporary Poets Celebrate the Diversity of Their Art, with Kathrine Varnes (2002)
After New Formalism: Poets on Form, Narrative, and Tradition (1999)
A Formal Feeling Comes: Poems in Form by Contemporary Women (1994)

Nirala Series

A Series of Contemporary Writing

Lost Horoscope *& Other New Poems*
Yuyutsu Sharma
ISBN 978-8195781638 pp. 72 Hardcover 2023 Rs. 495 Demy

A Short History of Nepal
From Ancient to Modern Times
Shreeram Prasad Upadhyaya
ISBN 978-8182500037 Rs. 595 pp Paperback 2022 Demy

A People's History of Nepal
Meena Ojha
ISBN 978-8195191543 pp 360 First Edition 2022 Paper Demy

Men's Lib and other literary, cultural and personal essays
Kumar Vikram
ISBN 978-81-9519-153-6 pp.260 2023 Paperback Demy

Shramatan: *A Nepalese Migrant Worker's Memoir*
BN Joshi
Translated from the Nepali by **Arun Budhathok**
ISBN 978-81-957816-5-2 Paperback 2023 Rs. 495 Demy

International Boundaries of Nepal
Buddhi Narayan Shrestha
ISBN 978-81-951915-7-4 pp 536 2022 Paper Demy

Hindu-Buddhist Festival of Nepal
Hemant K. Jha
ISBN: 978-8182500662 Paperback pp 204 2020 Demy

Kailash: Jewel of the Snows
Rajinder Arora
ISBN 978-8193936719 Paperback pp 268 pages with 68 colour

Indian Portraits: *Eight Christian Encounters with Hinduism*
Yann Vagneux
ISBN 978-81-951915-8-1 2021 Paperback

Dancing in Place: *New Poems*
S. Renay Sanders
ISBN ISBN 81-8250-048-6 2019 pp. 64 Paper Demy

Blue Fan Whirring : *Poems*
Mike Jurkovic
ISBN 978-8182500969 2019 pp. 160 Paper

The Second Buddha Walk: *Inspired by The Second Buddha , Master of Time Exhibit at Rubin Museum, New York*
Yuyutsu Sharma
ISBN 978-8182500983 2019 pp. 52 Paper Demy

Imagined Secrets: *New Poems*
Robert Scotto
ISBN 978-81825000442019 pp. 79 Paper Demy

The Tin Man
David B. Austell
ISBN 9-788182-500792 2019 pp. 320 Hard Demy

All Vows: *New & Selected Poems*
David B. Axelrod
ISBN 978-8182500822 2016 pp. 194 Paper Demy

The Dhimals: Miraculous Migrants of Himal:
An Anthropological Study of a Nepalese Ethnic Group
Murari P. Regmi
ISBN 9788182500082 2016 pp. 294 Paper Demy

A Blizzard In My Bones: New York Poems
Yuyutsu RD Sharma
ISBN 81-8250-070-2 2016 pp.134 Paper Demy

Letters from a Sacred Mountain Place: *A Journey through the Nepal Himalayas –Photographs and Text by* **Diane Frank**
ISBN 81-8250-095-8 2018 pp. 144 Hard Cover

Word Has It : *Poems*
Ruth Danon
ISBN 81-8250-097-4 2018 Paperback pp. 85 Demy

Eternal Snow: *A Worldwide Anthology of One Hundred Twenty Five Poetic Intersections with Himalayan Poet Yuyutsu RD Sharma*
Edited by **David Austell & Kathleen D Gallagher**
ISBN : 81-8250-088-5 2017 Paperback pp. 309 Demy

Cats, Love & Other Surprises
by **Otis Kidwell Burger**
Illustrations by **Katherine Burger**
ISBN : 978-8182500891 2017 Hardback pp. 65

Ritual: The Magical Perspective
Efficacy an the Search for Inner Meaning
Luc Sala
ISBN 9-788182-500617 2014 Hard pp. 832 Demy

Inside the Shell of the Tortoise
Poems written in India and Nepal (A Spanish English Edition)
Veronica Aranda
Translated by Claudia Routon with Yuyutsu Sharma
ISBN 9-788182-500686 2016 pp. 56 Hard Rs.395 Demy

Space Cake, Amsterdam *& Other Poems from Europe and America*
Yuyutsu RD Sharma
ISBN-81-8250-059-1 2014 Hard pp. 110

Milarepa's Bones, Helambu : *33 New Poems*
Yuyutsu RD Sharma
ISBN-81-8250-032-X 2012 Hard pp. 64 Demy

The Mystery Over Lord Buddha's Roots
An Analysis of the Mystery of the Shakya Kingdom
Mitsuaki KOJIMA
ISBN 9-788182-500563 2014 Hard pp. 165 Rs.495 Demy

Dada Poetry
An Introduction
William Seaton
Foreword by **Timothy Shipe**
ISBN-9-788182-500358 2013 Hard pp.112 Rs. 395 Demy

The Yeti
Spirit of Himalayan Forest Shamans
Larry G. Peters
ISBN 9-788182-500525 2014 Hard pp.128 Rs. 350 Demy

Folk Tales of Sherpa and Yeti
Collected by Shiva Dhakal
Adapted by Yuyutsu RD Sharma
ISBN 9-788182-500624 2014 Paper pp.125 Rs. 350 Demy

Annapurnas & Stains of Blood
Life, Travel &Writing on a page of Snow
Yuyutsu R D Sharma
ISBN 9-788182-500129 2010 Hard pp. 200 Rs. 495 Demy

Trance, Initiation & Psychotherapy in Nepalese Shamanism
Essays on Tamang and Tibetan Shamanism
Larry G.Peters
ISBN 9-788182-500532 2014 Paper pp. 412 Rs. 995 Demy

Tamang Shamans
An Ethnopsychiatric Study of Ecstasy and Healing in Nepal
Larry G. Peters
ISBN 9-788182-500099 2007 Paper pp. 179 Rs. 295 Demy

The Pokhara Valley
A Traveler's Guide
ISBN 9-788182-500198 2010 Paper pp. 202 Rs. 595 Demy